Values and Leadership

Anne Gold

**INSTITUTE OF
EDUCATION**
UNIVERSITY OF LONDON

First published in 2004 by the Institute of Education, University of London,
20 Bedford Way, London WC1H 0AL
www.ioe.ac.uk/publications

Over 100 years of excellence in education

British Library Cataloguing in Publication Data:
A catalogue record for this publication is available from the British Library

ISBN 0 85473 704 9

Design by Tim McPhee
Page make-up by Cambridge Photosetting Services, Cambridge

Production services by
Book Production Consultants plc, Cambridge

Printed and Bound By Cromwell Press, Trowbridge, Witshire

Contents

Acknowledgements

With thanks to Jennifer Evans, Marianne Coleman and Peter Earley for their generous comments and guidance.

1 Introduction

How can school leaders work in a way that is congruent with their own professional understandings and beliefs about learning and teaching? How can they be sure that the decisions they make are ethically in accord with their educational principles despite (or sometimes because of) the external demands that are constantly made on educational organisations? Our research shows that in the UK school leaders who are universally seen as good managers and leaders can work more autonomously and more in tune with their own educational values than we might have expected.

> Educational leadership ... is everything that consciously seeks to accomplish educational projects.
>
> (Hodgkinson 1991: 17)
>
> *leadership:* the process of guiding followers in a certain direction in pursuit of a vision, mission or goals; making and implementing and evaluating policy.
> *leader:* a person who exercises power, authority and influence over a group derived both from his or her acceptance by the group, and his or her position in the formal organization.
>
> (Oldroyd *et al.* 1996: 37)

This publication will take the reader through:

- Some working definitions of 'leadership' and 'values'.
- A personal example of how values around education have evolved but have basically stayed the same over one professional career.
- The argument that, despite the tumult surrounding education at the moment in England and in several other countries, those who make the opportunity to articulate their own values about education and about leadership in education are likely to make better informed and more profoundly professional decisions. Clearly articulated values leave a leader less likely to vacillate between different orthodoxies and more able to respond thoughtfully and in keeping with their own underpinning understandings of education.
- Research to show what such values might look like in practice and how they seem to overarch state initiatives about schooling.
- The tensions to be managed while leaders in educational organisations work towards agreeing values.
- Some strategies for building and sharing these values with others.
- Some suggestions for leaders about finding the space to articulate their own values.

Scattered throughout the text there are some boxed suggestions for activities or for further reading. You may wish to ignore them, or you may use them to engage further with the text and to explore the links between your own values and your professional practice.

There are international differences between the descriptors used for school leaders and the work they do. In the US, school leaders are often called 'principals' and their task is usually described as administration. In the UK, they are 'headteachers' and the task is thought to vary between leadership and management. In other parts of Europe, they may be 'rektors', 'school leaders', 'principals', 'skolastjori' or 'rehtori', and their management task varies according to the way that education is understood in each country.

Here, I use the term 'school leader' because that best describes both the structural, or power, position and the work done, and because it seems to be the most easily

---

Some definitions of values and leadership

Neither the culture of a school, nor the educational philosophy it espouses, is values-free. Both culture and philosophy have considerable effects upon the thinking and practices of the inhabitants of such institutions...all managers must be critically aware of the assumptions underlying [management], for it is only by being aware of and understanding them that one can really understand how schooling will affect the future ethical and political development of the people within the school and society at large.

(Bottery 1992)

Broad tendencies to prefer certain states of affairs over others.
The main cultural differences among nations lie in values. Systematic differences exist with regard to values about power and inequality, with regard to the relationships between the individual and the group, with regard to the social roles expected from men or women, with respect to ways of dealing with the uncertainties in life, and with respect to whether one is mainly preoccupied with the future or with the past and the present.'

(Hofstede 1994: 263)

Values are concerned with beliefs about moral or ethical matters. They exist as judgements. They are not the result of cold appraisal. Values are not deduced logically from a set of axioms – they are the axioms. We may agree with the writers of the American constitution when talking of values: 'We regard these truths as self-evident'. They are felt and believed. They are intensely human and vary widely between people. Values are often deeply held but they are not necessarily rational. ...You have already formed most of those you will ever have. You probably formed many of them almost unconsciously.

(National College for School Leadership (NCSL) 2002: 10)

Authentic leadership may be thought of as a metaphor for professionally effective, ethically sound, and consciously reflective practices in educational administration.

(Begley 2003: 1)

All leaders consciously or unconsciously employ values as guides to interpreting situations and suggesting appropriate administrative action. This is the artistry of leadership.

(Begley 2003: 11)

internationally recognised term. I take a leader to be anyone whose focus is generally on the learning and teaching in an educational organisation, and specifically on the development and delivery of learning and teaching through other professionals. In the UK, this means that they may be within the school, leading a section or a curriculum, pastoral or age phase, or they may be at the head of the school with responsibility for the whole organisation. Our research and many of the threads running through this work refer mainly to those who have overall responsibility for an educational institution, but the ideas and arguments are certainly of relevance to those who lead sectors within the organisation.

In this publication, therefore, I take 'values' to signify the core beliefs about life and about relating to other people that underpin understandings, principles and ethics about education and, here, about the leadership of education. There are different sets of values: the research done on effective leadership shows that different leadership styles and different understandings about leadership can be equally successful. However, the key set of values that drives the decisions of a school leader is concern with an understanding of the nature of power relations. Empowerment, democracy, equity and inclusion are all linked with power distribution and all depend on values and relationships.

> European society is structured in such a way as to ensure various overlapping sites of initial disadvantage and disempowerment. Western European society privileges those who are adult male, white, middle-class, able-bodied and heterosexual. So, women, children, people from ethnic minorities, working-class, aged, homosexual and disabled people do not naturally have access to positions of power or decision-making: they usually have to struggle harder to find a voice. And if they come from multiple sites of disadvantage – women from ethnic minorities, or working-class and disabled men, for example – their attempts to have access to cultural capital or the normal resources of a 'developed' society are even more fraught with difficulty. This positioning is often very subtle and hard to articulate – strong discourses of normality prevail which compound and reconfirm marginalization. Those who are marginalized often do not realise that they are disempowered – the strength of the discourse is such that many exclusions from power are taken for granted as natural. An ethical headteacher is aware of this, for both staff and students in a school, and will take steps to empower those who are societally disadvantaged.
>
> (Gold and Evans 1998: 10)

If a school leader understands that in order to lead well they must have a clear understanding of power relations, then a commitment to working well with issues of social justice will probably be the value that underpins all other leadership values. By this, I mean that there will be no doubt that everyone in the school community must be able to access and take part in the learning and teaching, and that it is acknowledged that different life journeys and previous access to the locus of power will affect how each person takes part.

I know that I display my own values here and in the next section. It is difficult to write about values in a way that sets out alternatives and choices because when writing I am so affected by what I believe is the right way to be. I find it almost impossible to be non-judgemental, because my values even inform the choices I made about what to include and use in this publication and what to leave out. And I am sure that the two teams in which I did the research described in Chapter 4 were led by our collective values when we chose our research methods, gathered and then analysed the resultant data.

I am trying not to introduce these values about leadership and education as the only acceptable set of values. I intend this publication to show *how* school leaders' values are constructed, articulated and worked with, not *which* values *should* be displayed. Our research uncovered different sets of values. I will try to show the structures and questions around the values we saw, posing useful questions rather than imposing one set of beliefs about life.

2 *Professional values evolve*

A PERSONAL ACCOUNT

In this section, I am going to describe my own values evolution in order to illustrate the way that I think, on the whole, values adapt but stay fundamentally the same.

I have been working in 'education' for more than 40 years: in September 1963 I entered a three-year primary teachers' training course at the University of London, Goldsmiths' College. I am now a senior lecturer in educational leadership and management at the Institute of Education, University of London. My values about education and subsequently about leading and managing in education have evolved during this time – like most people, the beliefs and vision that moved me at 18 have affected many of my later decisions in life, but they have slowly become more realistic, more achievable and probably not as noble or pure. *In other words they have been affected by my changing understanding of the world around me.*

COMING TO CONSCIOUSNESS

I think that I first woke up to the outside world around the time of the Sharpeville massacre (1960) and the Cuban missile crisis (1962). Among the books and films that influenced me at that time were *To Sir with Love* by E.R. Braithwaite, *On the Beach* by Nevil Shute and *The Blackboard Jungle* (a film released in 1955). I was advised to teach by my school – that was what girls did then if they did not go into the bank or into nursing. I did not want to teach, but I wanted to change the world, or at least to stop it from exploding. For some reason I can't remember now, I worked in a primary school for three weeks, and I fell in love with teaching!

> I didn't sleep properly in seven years. When I left the class of children of whom I had grown the fondest of all, I wrote a poem (all the bad, abandoned poems)... It was a poem about affection: all our bondage is bought by the soft pressure of fingers, the child's arms slipped unthinkingly around the adult's waist, the head resting, momentarily listening to a heart-beat.
>
> (Carolyn Steedman 1985)

I finally decided to go into teaching (at 19) because I thought it might be a way to try to make things better – *I thought that teaching was a way to help people to make informed choices about their lives.*

BEGINNING TEACHING

Primary teacher training in the mid-1960s was above all child-centred. Our reading included Jean-Jacques Rousseau's *Émile*, where the young boy was encouraged to roam free and learn from nature, and versions of the works of Freud where we were taught that it is unnecessary and may even be repressively damaging to put curbs and boundaries round the free expression of young children. We learnt that when children were motivated and ready, they would read automatically and they would be ceaselessly eager to explore their worlds. *We were encouraged to put learners and learning at the centre of our work – they led us. This linked with encouraging people to make informed choices because the focus was now on the learner rather than the teacher.*

TWENTY YEARS' TEACHING AND MANAGING IN INNER-LONDON SECONDARY SCHOOLS

During 20 years working as a special needs teacher in inner-London comprehensive schools, I came to develop a deeper understanding of the sociological context for learning and teaching. Initially I thought that many of the children with whom I worked were already positioned by society to fail educationally, and I believed that I should relate to them principally pastorally and through counselling. I still believed that when they understood their worlds better they could make more informed choices, and that they would choose to become successful learners and good citizens. I was not, however, sure that I could do anything to change their worlds for them. My final years as a schoolteacher were spent as a middle manager/leader, and then a senior manager/leader. I then came to see that I needed to focus on learning and to encourage young people who were challenging to focus on their own learning. I was now able to work through other teachers to make the learning environment more positive for challenging young people. *I still put learners at the centre of my work, but I learnt that I needed to take more responsibility for their learning than I initially thought was necessary. I thought that I could probably help them to make a difference to their worlds.*

BEING HERE – WORKING IN A HIGHER EDUCATION INSTITUTION

I came to the Institute of Education to teach about leadership and management. I now believe that educational leaders can encourage young people to make informed choices. Leaders model their values to all those in their learning community – their values are constantly on display. By working in a principled and values-driven way with the adult professionals around them, *they can to some extent change the worlds around learners in order to ensure that their learning helps them to make informed choices.*

I think I can trace my values and beliefs about education from my 18-year-old self, but those beliefs have been modified by my subsequent life experiences, including studying and talking, which have afforded me the opportunities to revisit my values and beliefs.

> Here you may wish to trace the connections between your own professional journey and the development of your values. Have they changed? Are they still connected? Do you think about them?

③ *Clearly articulated values*

Those educational leaders who take the opportunity to articulate their own values about education and about leadership in education despite the tumult surrounding education at the moment in several countries, are likely to make better informed and more profoundly professional decisions. Clearly articulated values leave a leader less likely to vacillate between different political and educational orthodoxies and more able to respond thoughtfully.

THINKING ABOUT VALUES

Often when I work with educational leaders, I ask them a set of linked questions, to be answered alone:

1. Why did they originally decide to work in education?
2. What are their underpinning values at present about education? (This is a private thought that they do not share with others.)
3. Is there a linkage between their initial entry into education and their present values about education?
4. Are their values about education linked to, and affecting, their leadership styles?

In other words, I offer them the opportunity to think about their values about education and about leadership in education, and to think about the links between their values and their leadership practice.

> You may wish to link your previous answers (about your professional journey and the development of your values) with your leadership style: are they connected?

I am struck by the way the educational leaders with whom I am working respond *physically* to these questions. They often begin by sitting and writing notes shyly and hesitatingly. As they draw out their own values, in a room away from their organisation and without having to share them with others, they tend to sit up straight and they seem more grounded and more eager to talk about profound issues. Apparently they see these questions initially as intrusive and difficult, but ultimately their body language shows answering them to be confirming and liberating. Their busy professional lives make such demands on their time that they rarely have the opportunity for this level of professional reflection. I see it as part of my task as an academic working in the field of educational leadership to offer them such opportunities. Their physical responses to the opportunity show how important this opportunity is.

CAPTURING THE LEADERSHIP DISCOURSE There are writers in the fields of educational policy sociology and educational leadership who believe that it is impossible to maintain a core set of values about education that is unaffected by the state and by other challenges to the autonomy of school leaders. Indeed, I wrote above that my life experiences have modified my values and beliefs. Such writers pay particular attention, for example, to the challenges and subsequent modifications to leadership values which seem to come from a global move towards 'new managerialism' in public sector organisations. Nigel Wright (2001) uses the term 'bastard leadership' to show the way that key responsibility for the task of educational leadership has been disputed and changed by the managerialism that is now demanded from school leaders in the UK.

> Leadership as the moral and value underpinning for the direction of schools is being removed from those who work there. It is now very substantially located at the political level where it is not available for contestation, modification or adjustment to local variations.
>
> (Wright 2001: 280)

Wright's writing is built upon the inevitability of the usurpation of free will in educational leaders so that there is a 'subtle capturing of the leadership discourse' by governments, civil servants, leadership developers and researchers alike.

I came across a recent example of the way ideas are 'captured' and then described in unusual and powerful language when working as a school governor in an Ofsted report:

> Inspectors must evaluate and report on the quality of leadership of the school, particularly by the headteacher, senior team and other staff with responsibilities, assessing the extent to which leadership shows a clear vision, a sense of purpose and high aspirations for the school, with *relentless* focus on pupils' achievement.
>
> (Ofsted 2003: 46; my emphasis)

I use italics here to give an example of 'capturing a discourse': *'relentless'* is not normally a word to be connected with the moral high ground in education, but doubtless it will soon be commonly used as a positive word. It will become common usage to describe the way that teachers will work tirelessly to improve learning and teaching in their schools.

> What other words or phrases introduced within government initiatives have you first been surprised by, then used yourself within quotation marks, and ultimately used freely and without irony as part of your regular professional discussions?

MAINTAINING AUTONOMY OF VALUES For several years now, I have been working with colleagues at the Institute of Education, University of London on research about school leadership. Our writing and research, and indeed this publication, set out to show that although the pressure on school leaders to conform is enormous, there are ways to maintain an autonomy of central values which shape their responses to government demands about education. Chapter 4 takes the reader through two pieces of our research about educational leadership and values which, we hope, show this.

Wright says that the multiplicity of tasks demanded by the state limits school leaders' autonomy. He sees the state initiatives that drive education in England today as usually ill-informed or based on poor research.

It is actually about the lack of scope for school leaders to make decisions that legitimately fly in the face of particular unrealistic and often inadequately researched government initiatives or requirements.

(Wright 2003: 140)

The daily work of educational leaders, in the UK at least, is now made up of the need for fast reactions; the effective management of large budgets and of diverse groups of adults and children; and the ability to relate productively to the outside world as well as to the internal minutiae of the organisation. School leaders in the UK also need to respond to legal and governmental demands, to lead policy implementation and strategically successful long-term planning and above all to ensure good learning and teaching. They are expected to do so at high speed because consultation processes in England are often expected to be completed in short time windows, or because the offer of extra funding for specific projects is for a limited period.

It is true that the multi-layered nature of the work and the haste of responses expected mean that it is easy to make mistakes of judgement. Speed limits judgement and closes down options so that the temptation is to make easy choices, or to make decisions that have been made often before, without fresh examination. However, the key to autonomy is to be able to get in touch with already clarified or articulated values, so that new decisions may be measured against them.

To put it very bluntly, the educational enterprise does not always know where it is going, or what it is actually accomplishing, or even how to do what is supposed to be its primary task – the teaching-learning process. From an objective standpoint it is not at all clear to what extent teaching methodology is traditionalized ritual as opposed to scientific technology …

Yet these very difficulties are the source of peculiar leadership opportunities: the opportunity to discover, clarify and defend the ends of education, to motivate towards those ends; the opportunity to discover means and invent process, since the prevalent state of pedagogic science permits rather than constrains; and the opportunity to create and establish morally grounded evaluation and legitimate it for all the participants in the great cooperative educational project. All of which means that educational leadership is especially difficult, especially challenging and especially moral.

(Hodgkinson 1991: 62)

Since the publication of Hodgkinson's book in Canada the task of educational leadership has become far more complex in many parts of the world: the state has on the whole withdrawn from some of the daily decision-making in schools and universities, and has devolved financial power more directly to the educational organisations. However, at the same time national curricula have often been more firmly prescribed from the centre. Thus there is a tension between centralisation and the devolution of decision-making. This has changed the relationship of educational leaders to the state and to their communities. They have to manage more than 'the teaching-learning process' and are now working with large budgets and creative strategic plans, while responding more tightly to state policies about curriculum content, assessment and results. It is even more necessary, therefore, to find a calm or stillness at the centre of this pressure, so that sound decisions are made. Our research shows that many school leaders welcome the autonomy that devolved budgets have brought them. It is even more important, therefore, to make sure that the autonomy has ethical dimensions to it.

STANDARDS IN PUBLIC LIFE

There are yet more dimensions to the pressures on contemporary educational leaders. For example, in most countries, they are seen as community leaders. They have power and influence over the wide community of a school and the wider community served by the school. They are public figures with all the status responsibility that position brings with it. The Nolan Committee on Standards in Public Life (1996) was set up in the UK in an attempt to bring integrity back to public life. The Committee's report makes educative reading because it aims to offer a set of values by which to lead a principled life in public. It sets out seven principles for all who work in public positions. There seems to be a qualitative difference between 'honesty' and 'accountability' – the latter may be a way of ensuring the former. Nevertheless, these are important statements, especially as it is suggested that they underpin all public life – including those people working as school leaders.

Summary of the Nolan Committee's First Report on Standards in Public Life

The Seven Principles of Public Life

Selflessness
Holders of public office should take decisions solely in terms of the public interest. They should not do so in order to gain financial or other material benefits for themselves, their family, or their friends.

Integrity
Holders of public office should not place themselves under any financial or other obligation to outside individuals or organisations that might influence them in the performance of their official duties.

Objectivity
In carrying out public business, including making public appointments, awarding contracts, or recommending individuals for rewards and benefits, holders of public office should make choices on merit.

Accountability
Holders of public office are accountable for their decisions and actions to the public and must submit themselves to whatever scrutiny is appropriate to their office.

Openness
Holders of public office should be as open as possible about all the decisions and actions that they take. They should give reasons for their decisions and restrict information only when the wider public interest clearly demands.

Honesty
Holders of public office have a duty to declare any private interests relating to their public duties and to take steps to resolve any conflicts arising in a way that protects the public interest.

Leadership
Holders of public office should promote and support these principles by leadership and example.

These principles apply to all aspects of public life. The Committee has set them out here for the benefit of all who serve the public in any way.

http://www.archive.official-documents.co.uk/document/parlment/nolan/nolan.htm

Do you think that Nolan's seven principles of public life fit those who lead in education? Do they offer a useful way of thinking about school leadership? Are they a universal set of values, or one set of values-led principles?

School leaders whose leadership decisions are informed by professional values about leading learning and teaching have profound effects on the schools that they lead. Wright tells us that the professional judgement of school leaders is often affected adversely by the demands of new managerialism coming from new government initiatives. This is partly because of the speed at which changes are demanded, and partly because of the volume of change, so that there is little opportunity to match the changes to professionally informed values. However, Nolan is proposing a set of core values to underpin the work and the professional decisions of all public figures, and which have a measured reflection embedded in them.

4 *Research on leadership values in practice*

In many countries, there is a national curriculum for schools, usually legislated by the government of the day, and displaying the government's political values in the curriculum content. Political values are also evident in the looseness or tightness by which school leaders are controlled and monitored in their interpretation and implementation of the National Curriculum. The two pieces of research presented in this section both took place in England, during a period in which the Department for Education and Science (in variously changing titles) had closely prescribed the implementation and monitoring of the National Curriculum for more than ten years. Most of the school leaders interviewed had begun teaching when the curriculum in their schools was described through more professional autonomy, although national examination boards set the examination standards and thus the examination syllabuses.

It is important to note here that each of the leaders to whom we spoke (and there were 16 in all) expressed different values. The papers that arose from the research projects were not written to exemplify one way of working or one key set of values. Rather the papers focus on the values of the school leaders who were the subjects of the research. Both papers attempt to see whether the school leaders had expectations for their schools and those who learned in them that were added on to, or overarching, the expectations set by the English National Curriculum. Their expectations for their schools and for those who learned and taught in them were clearly different and sometimes, if set next to each other, would appear to be in opposition to each other. These papers, therefore, were not written to recommend one set of values. They were written to see whether the school leaders could easily articulate their values and, if so, how they did this and how they worked with them.

PRINCIPLED PRINCIPALS?

The first research project that I want to report on was based on ten case studies: I and my colleagues chose ten schools in England whose leadership had been highly rated by recent UK Office of Standards in Education [Ofsted] inspections, and then we confirmed the high quality with local education authority advisers. The project was reported in 'Principled principals? Values-driven leadership: evidence from ten case Studies of "Outstanding' School Leaders"' by Anne Gold, Jennifer Evans, Peter Earley, David Halpin and Pat Collarbone.

I want to make it clear here that we were not, at this point, asking about values. We were looking much more generally at good leadership. Only as we wrote up our case studies did it became clear that we were able to draw a picture of these ten outstanding school leaders who were undoubtedly translating their educational values into leadership practices.

As researchers *we* were able to make clear connections between the school leaders' values and their leadership, and they did often tell us about the schools' strong and shared value systems. Indeed, three of our interviewees used the name of their school as a descriptor for the way they do things, as in 'K...nites' who had absorbed the supportive and egalitarian ethos of the school, or the 'B... way of doing things' and the 'E... way' which was meant to denote a liberal, broad-based and inclusive approach to education. We were intrigued by the ways they worked to build these shared values – we looked for evidence of articulation and promotion so that the staff of the school would also know how the 'B... way of doing things' really worked.

In essence, we found that they all worked towards articulating and communicating values by:

- Working with, managing and even searching out change
- Keeping staff constantly informed
- Working closely with their senior management and leadership teams
- Developing leadership capacity and responsibility throughout the school.

These four main strategies (shared by all our case study schools) were the clearest examples of leadership in action which led us to describe the values of the leaders to whom we spoke. We took them as both indicators and implementers of underpinning leadership values. I will explain further how these four indicators of values looked in practice, as I introduce sections from the paper to illustrate the indicators.

Working with, managing and even searching out change

Earlier in this book, I referred to the tumult which is the backdrop to school leadership in England in the early twenty-first century. Schools are constantly on display, through the publications of large amounts of information about them in the public domain. At the same time, it has become accepted that learning and teaching will improve if adjustments are regularly made to the way education is delivered, also indeed to what aspects of education are delivered. Some of the changes are supported by legislation, and others are a result of different financial rewards and projects – school leaders are regularly asked to bid for different types of short-term funding to back up change in their schools. Bids for funding have to be written persuasively and at speed – bid writing has become an important leadership skill.

We found that the school leaders we were following were working quite consciously with change. They were clear about which changes fitted their values, and they rejected those changes which, they felt, would lead them away from their core purpose as a school. They did not always see change as a negative force, however – they managed change in such a way as to keep their educational values alive, supporting their journey towards their ultimate goals, and seeking out change when they thought that their school needed to be running on a different track or at a different speed.

In the paper, we wrote:

> *Several of the school leaders were generally proactive in their attitude for change, although for reportedly different reasons: one was good at 'environmental scanning', in order to anticipate 'what is coming along and preparing ourselves for it, so that when it does happen it's not such a shock'. Another told us 'if you don't do something different, you won't move on'. A member of staff told us in yet another school that the school leader was 'good at saying "Let's take the good bits"', but was reluctant to take up the latest government initiative (in this case, that of becoming a professional development or 'Beacon' school) because it was felt that one more initiative might cause them to 'take their eye off the ball'. We also heard about a school which had taken on several new initiatives where the school leader explained to us that the new initiatives 'make the school feel good about itself and give people a chance to raise their own game and learn'. Yet another school leader in our investigation used ICT to research and bring back new ideas to the school.*
>
> *Several of those we interviewed described the process of mediating new initiatives through the school's value systems as a reflective activity shared by all the staff: 'We're never stagnant ... it's because we never really leave things that long without review ... we're questioning all the time, it's constant review'. Another school leader, who*

believed that 'change must be at the shop-floor if it is to be effective' and was seen by the staff and governors as a visionary, told us that he did not believe in change for change's sake – not all initiatives were considered to be good for the school, but all must go through a filtering process of 'a healthy disrespect for change'. A school leader of a nursery and infants school told us how she protected her staff from multiple innovations by filtering external demands to try to ensure that 'we do what we think is best for our children' – she thought that the self-confidence and assurance that had grown during her leadership tenure ensured that she was not 'jumping simply because someone tells you to jump'. (p. 130)

The school leaders we spoke to described mediating change, negotiating it effectively and adapting it to fit their values. They were not resistant to change: some of them welcomed it, and all of them managed it. Indeed the very process of change mediation was seen as a way of bringing staff together to articulate shared values and it also meant that the school leaders were in charge of the change.

Keeping staff constantly informed

This research finding is completely data-driven: we asked about decision-making within the schools, and as we listened to the responses, we realised that the school leaders consciously worked with information as a clearly values-led activity. They acknowledged that their staff needed information in order to contribute to effective decision-making. We realised that the amount of information made available to staff was dependent on the school leaders' understandings about informed and democratic decision-making. They linked how much information to make available to the school community with the extent to which they wished them to be involved with decision-making.

In the paper we wrote:

School leaders and other staff in our case studies gave us many examples of how meetings and information were seen as important: in one special school, we heard how teamwork was fostered and facilitated through meetings of the whole staff, team meetings and a programme of individual discussions between the school leader and all members of staff. The free flow of information within the school was referred to by many members of staff and was seen as contributing to the spirit of togetherness and the inhibition of any feeling of 'them and us'. In this school, good communication was not left to chance – there were systems in place such as the staff-room notice board, the circulation of minutes of meetings and the weekly staff briefings in order to ensure that information and ideas were freely shared.

In a large secondary school, we observed a woman school leader showing her respect for her colleagues through the way she ran meetings: she constantly invited them to contribute their views, building consensus round the discussion and generally building agreement through the discussion. In another large secondary school, teachers were encouraged to conduct research and enquiry, and most staff appeared to share a thirst for knowledge and enquiry in the school.

In a smaller school, the school leader used several strategies for encouraging a shared sense of purpose: staff meetings for discussions and review 'where we review things like what you say, what you do...'; a termly agenda-setting staff handbook which also includes 'little articles ... depends on what the focus of the term is, or whether we've got problems or where we've got weaknesses'; and his way of spreading the use of ICT among his staff – 'we've just been given laptops – all the teachers. The Head's ... putting planning sheets and school end of year reports and annual reviews, and everything's on it.' (p. 133)

They all saw meetings as key information-giving and decision-making spaces. Meetings are an unusually visible way of displaying a leader's values system. If a researcher wishes to see leadership values in action, it is revealing to observe how a school leader chairs a meeting. The leader's values may be read through:

- how the agenda is shaped
- who can speak
- who is heard
- whose opinions are sought
- how decisions are made
- whether consensus is sought.

These are all indicators of power relations. A leader who understands power relations and who works towards using them to either frame consensus or to impose future actions is making their values visible to those they lead. If consensus is sought and everyone at the meeting understands that they have a voice and that they are working towards consensus, they will take part in the meeting very differently from how they would in one in which they know that they are there to accept what they are told to do, with little discussion.

We were interested to see other ways in which the school leaders kept their staff informed. One school leader in particular caught our attention by the way he worked with technology. He was the head of a special school, thus of quite a small staff, and he gave each member of the teaching staff a laptop computer, onto which he had programmed several school-specific files and spreadsheets. His staff found this very helpful. He also downloaded key research and articles each month, which he then passed on to his staff in an easily readable form. He found ways of keeping them professionally informed which did not overload them, but which gave them key points for 'learning conversations' (Brookfield 1987: 238).

Those school leaders who decide that it is important to keep their staff informed are sharing power in a way that those who do not appear to trust their staff with information are not. Easy access to information encourages autonomy and easier decision-making. It also encourages professional discussion, so that staff can work towards shared values and values-informed activity.

Working closely with their senior management and leadership teams

We were struck by the way that the school leaders we studied worked with the power relationships thrown up by hierarchy. By this, I mean that although almost every one of them seemed to work towards building a strong, effective and active leadership team, they made sure that the team was accessible by the rest of the school, so that they both listened to and were heard by their less senior colleagues. The leadership team was thus 'permeable'.

The financial background to this teamwork is that in England, senior leaders or managers in schools are paid a considerably higher salary than those who remain in the classroom, or those middle managers or leaders who have responsibility for specific sections of the curriculum. They also spend less time in the classroom and more time planning strategically for the future of the school and in order to lead the organisation – in these ways they move away from the daily life of most teaching professionals who work in the school, and who are often concerned with different agendas. It is easy for senior leaders to become distant from their colleagues and even to feel so separate from them that a lack of trust develops along with a different set of values, because the different professional focuses seem so disparate. Some leaders appear to become so concerned with managing the organisation that they lose sight of the learning and teaching which is at the heart of a school.

In this paper we wrote:

> *Our case studies showed teams that were seen as strong, but consulting, respectful and listening. They managed to be separate enough to lead the school, but accessible*

enough to know how the school community wanted to be led. The deputy head of a large primary school remarked that the school's senior management team worked well together: 'we're all pulling in the same direction, sharing the same values'. The staff of that school held the head and deputy in very high esteem. Indeed, the relationship of mutual respect between the leadership team and the rest of the staff in the schools we studied was strikingly similar (p. 131).

Another point we raised as we compared our research findings was that as researchers, it was not always easy, or even possible, to read the interpersonal dynamics within the senior leadership team. When we raised this with the people we interviewed, they could not tell us where ideas arose because the teams worked together so smoothly.

For example, the head of a special school commented: 'It's a bit like a machine – it's my job in particular to come up with good ideas, or to encourage the deputy head and the senior co-ordinator to come up with good ideas'. Another member of the staff of that school told us: 'the head and deputy head are the school leadership … the SMT is important, ultimately the headteacher is the boss, he makes the final decisions, he is responsible … it's on his shoulders'. It was easier to trace the decision-making processes in this school because although the principal worked creatively with his senior management team to 'come up with good ideas', he ultimately took and was seen as taking, the final responsibility. However, in separate conversations with the school leader and his deputy, both of them stated that they did not always know which of them brought the new ideas to the SMT.

A large nursery and infants school we visited was led by a head and deputy head, neither of whom had a teaching timetable at that time (other than releasing colleagues). Both were highly visible around the school, they got on very well with each other and worked closely together as the senior management team. The rest of the staff saw them as strong and purposeful: 'you don't feel threatened by the leadership here – you're moved forward and in a positive way'. It was clear that she and her deputy worked very closely and were often almost interchangeable in their instructional leadership activities.

In an inner-city large primary school, the senior management team was made up of talented and committed teachers with high energy, where there was an over-riding ethos of consultation between the members of that team and between staff. It seems that this relationship was fostered by the school leader's beliefs and management style: 'a very personal type of leader. He practices what he preaches. He doesn't say one thing and do another. He knows everybody and will go above and beyond the call of duty' (p. 132).

Members of staff commented on the attention school leaders paid to the way their senior leadership teams communicated with and listened to the rest of the school. They welcomed the fine balance between leading and listening, and between consulting and making decisions. Both of these careful positions are informed by values-led thinking about consultation, democracy and the recognition of colleagues' professional knowledge.

Developing leadership capacity and responsibility throughout the school

Some recent writing about leadership in schools has presented the concept of 'distributed' leadership. This could mean that the responsibility for the leadership and management tasks of a school is shared throughout the school in order to make sure that the school runs efficiently and that more work is done. But it could also be used to describe a more democratic and educative way of sharing leadership.

All the leaders to whom we spoke paid serious attention to the development of leadership capacity throughout their schools, in a way that we thought showed their underpinning values about democracy. The school leaders recognised that their middle leaders –

> Helen Gunter describes 'distributed leadership' as having: 'less to do with managerial efficiency and more to do with educational leadership working within and developing a democracy'.
>
> Gunther (2001: 131)

curriculum leaders, pastoral leaders and subject heads – were indeed more expert in their specialist field than the school leaders were themselves. And they encouraged this recognition of expertise in other members of staff. This school leadership respect for the knowledge of subject leaders is echoed in the description of a values clash which is to be found at the beginning of Chapter 5.

They made sure that members of staff were constantly upgrading their knowledge, and they sometimes sponsored young or (to us) surprisingly inexperienced members of staff to become middle leaders before the less senior teachers had themselves thought of promotion. We linked the support for leadership throughout the schools with the school leaders' encouragement of professional development throughout the school.

In the paper we wrote:

> *We make the connection here between expecting expertise from middle managers and supporting them and other staff members with forms of training and development (such as reflective conversations, networking, role models and mentors) that are much wider and more informal than in-service courses, but which set up an ethos or culture where school leaders are prepared to take risks and to create a safe environment for others to do so (pp. 132–3)*

The school leaders encouraged leadership capacity throughout the school, but made sure that they backed up that leadership development with a notable culture of supportive professional development.

This is a description of our work on ten case studies of outstanding headteachers – from our research data, we were able to offer accounts of some of the leadership values in action. We were sometimes able to see quite small or detailed interactions which clearly signified profound values.

> This research-based article picked out four ways of seeing leadership values in action. What might a visitor to your school pick as evidence of your leadership and educational values?

LEADERSHIP VALUES IN ACTION

In order to do our research for the second project, my co-authors and I spoke at length to six school leaders about the values that underpin their work in schools. Our findings were published in 'Articulating leadership values in action: conversations with school leaders', by Carol Campbell, Anne Gold and Ingrid Lunt. There is more research to be done about the reality of school leaders' values – how they talk about their values, and whether it is possible to see the links, the outcomes, and the evidence of leadership values in normal daily classroom interactions. This paper is one part of that research – how do school leaders express their values, and what do those values influence? We plan ultimately to look at the classroom to see how those values translate into practice and whether they leave an evidence trail – whether it is possible to see how they influence classroom practice.

For this paper, therefore, unlike the previous paper, we *did* ask about the school leaders' perceptions of leadership and their expressions of values – here, we did not focus on their actual leadership practice. We asked them about:

- the links between their values and their leadership styles
- the values that informed the school ethos
- the extent to which their own values affected the school ethos
- how much they were influenced by the local community
- how they thought the school values had effects on the students, inside and outside the classroom.

> How might *you* answer these questions?

From the answers to these questions, we were able to see that the school leaders to whom we spoke described their values as being influential on:

- what they wanted for the young people in their schools
- their management of their staff
- how they managed relationships with the community in and around the school.

Below, I expand these influences further.

What school leaders wanted for the young people in their schools

We found that although it was important to all the school leaders that the young people in their schools attained as far as possible in nationally examined terms, none of them saw pupil achievement and outcomes in purely measurable terms of attainment. Their values about education led them to expect more than this for the learners in the schools they led.

Indeed, the values they articulated to us were over and above the current UK government standards agenda – they certainly wanted the young people to 'do well' in orthodox and measurable attainment terms, but they also all spoke about different aspects of personal development. They referred to 'high expectations', 'self-esteem' and 'empowering' when describing their school cultures. They were committed to educational opportunity and social justice, and they used language such as 'social inclusion', 'valuing diversity' and 'equality of opportunity' to explain their school ethos further.

It was interesting to note that they spoke to us about high standards of classroom management and codes of behaviour and about empowering students through exciting learning. These are common phrases used in current discourses of learning and teaching. But they were used in our interviews as vehicles for the 'expanded' dimensions, as values added on to the standards agenda.

In this paper, we wrote:

> *Overall, the school leaders articulated a strongly held set of developmental and educational values which they believed informed their leadership approach to working with students. While the UK government's emphasis on standards, particularly attainment and behaviour, had some resonance with the school leaders' values, these were articulated broadly and in combination with a wider set of developmental and educational values.*

We know that we did not ascertain, in this research, whether the school leaders ensured that the schools they led actually delivered learning and teaching which displayed these values. We were, however, clear that the practices and decisions, which were led by the school leaders within the schools, were informed by these values.

Management of staff

Between them the six school leaders described quite a broad spectrum of chosen leadership styles which were, of course, informed by their (different) values. They used phrases such as 'facilitative management' and 'shared decision-making', but all of them were ultimately ready to take the final decisions themselves. They spoke about their values both in how they related to the staff with whom they worked, and in their recruitment practices for new staff.

They discussed the relationship between their values and those of the staff with whom they work, at length: this is clearly a serious issue for school leaders and I explore it further in Chapter 5. One of the school leaders to whom we spoke stressed the importance of articulating her values and discussing these with her staff. She hoped she conveyed her values in her actions, and she clearly expected that the staff with whom she worked knew generally how she would behave in any situation.

The school leaders differed in how much they tolerated differences in values in those who worked in the school, in how they worked with that difference, and in the extent to which they tried to persuade staff to share their values. One school leader described how she worked individually with different members of staff, building up a core of people who shared values with her, and expecting that core to spread those values out to other staff members. Another leader told us that she was able to tolerate dissension, but that she was ready to take the lead when necessary.

As in the previous paper, all these school leaders commented on the importance of professional development for staff in their schools. The development took different forms – from individual discussions to meetings and to collaborative work through regular workshops and international research projects – but all the school leaders saw professional development as an important means of empowering the staff.

There was a common allusion to the expectation that members of the Senior Management Team shared leadership responsibilities and were seen to share values. We were told about the construction of the Senior Management Team to include members with different strengths and weaknesses, but with an expectation that they would promote shared values.

In the paper, we wrote:

> *although the values articulated for staff are similar to those articulated for students in terms of stressing personal and educational development, the school leaders indicated also the importance of developing a leadership and management relationship which promoted their values as shared values across the staff. It was not simply the specification of values that was important, but also their distribution and identification by staff.*

Management of relationships with the community in and around the school

All the school leaders took account of the community served by and serving the schools. We were intrigued to hear which aspects they chose to tell us about the communities, and we decided that this choice was values-driven.

We wrote:

> *All the school leaders took their local community into account, and all had ways of describing their relationship with those around the school. In some cases this was presented as an understanding of 'race' issues, social disadvantage and social inclusion; sometimes we were told about working with parents to parent more effectively; and often we heard descriptions of the ways in which different communities had been encouraged by the school to be less hostile and more tolerant of each other.*

The school leaders told us that it was important to be involved in the local community. They spoke about how their own values influenced their relationship with parents: one of them was clear that part of his leadership role was to engage parents in developing further their parenting skills and even to try to encourage them to parent in a way he could approve of. Others talked about the way religious, ethnic and socio-economic characteristics of the local communities influence processes and practices within the schools – they involved the parents, while being aware that some of them may have difficulties engaging with education and schooling. Here is another example of school leaders who have to work with some conflicting values, this time in relationship to the community. They had to mediate between the community influences which came into their schools and the influence they wanted to have in order to change practices in the community around the school.

We wrote:

And while Mr D believes that he is making 'slow progress' to engage parents, Ms F points out the existence of conflict when the headteacher's values may extend to how parents should behave:

'Yes I do get angry parents who resent what I say and the values I hold like getting up in the morning with your child, you know that is what mums do, don't just let them lie in bed.'

The headteacher's values and role therefore may influence their relationships with parents. Thus while these headteachers and schools may be central to the local community, they are also separate from that community. For example, trying to encourage vocational aspirations in an area of unemployment:

'....there is still a lot of difficulty out there against the situation where you are working towards vocational aspirations and many of the children that we are working with go home each day to a home that has never had experience of anybody having employment.' (Mr D)

Or acting against racism in a multicultural community and school:

'We are definitely in a community which is rather than multicultural, well it is multicultural but largely bicultural because we have two very large ethnic groups: a traditional white working class group and then a Bangladeshi community and then very small numbers of others, so it is unusual in that sense.... So a very important part of the ethos is our commitment to equal opportunities. Obviously we are committed to that but a very specific thing about working here is a tradition of racism in this community. So a very important [aim] of this school is trying to get young people to work together, to understand each other, to have relationships with each other, to trust each other across an ethnic divide.... I suspect when we get that right it also supports the impact on exam results ... we are in a community which is in many ways quite a divided, it is a very divided community and there is a lot of tension so that impinges on our work.' (Mr B)

The school therefore has a role in educating students and the wider community and in providing different 'community' values from those surrounding the school.

The first paper in this section set out to show how school leaders' values played out in reality – how their leadership in action allowed observers to read the values which underpinned their actions. The second paper described the sites that the next set of school leaders chose as evidence of their values – they told us what main arenas in the leadership of their schools were most influenced by their values.

In this chapter I have linked the rhetoric of values to the reality of leadership. I have presented the papers in such detail to show research findings about the links between values and actions. The next chapter lays out the complexity school leaders manage when trying to bring the organisation towards shared values while encouraging independence and individual values.

5 *Organisational tensions in agreeing*

values

This chapter takes a recurring theme from the (previous) research chapter: how do school leaders work with different sets of values within the school, or between the school and the community. In other words, how much complexity and difference of values can they tolerate? Is this tolerance a values-informed area?

MANAGING CONFLICTING VALUES: A CASE STUDY

I begin with an illustration of a common problem: a school in which the school leader manages a serious clash of values. The dilemma for this school leader lies in balancing her values about equity with her values about democracy. This must be a common dilemma for school leaders who try to work within a democratic framework.

The school in the case study below is an amalgam of several different inner city schools in the UK:

This is a school for boys and girls set in a large city. The students are aged 11–16, and they come from many different ethnic groupings. The predominant student group is of African origin, but there are also young people from South Asia, Eastern Europe and the Mediterranean. By all state indicators, this school is set in a 'deprived ' part of the city: the majority of young people in the school do not have English as their mother tongue, and a high proportion of them are on free school dinners (two indicators used by the UK government to describe schools as 'in challenging circumstances').

However, the school's recently published examination and Key stage 3 and 4 results are so impressive that the school has been deemed to be in the country's top 5 per cent of improving schools. There is a clear sense of community in the school; a calm, purposeful and good-tempered culture; and the teachers tend to stay there for most of their teaching careers, giving the school stability and wisdom.

The school leader was previously a deputy leader in the school. She has now led the school for seven years. Originally, her teaching subject was science, although she no longer teaches. She has taken a decision that she and her leadership team should absorb the strategic planning and bureaucracy necessary to keep the school functioning so effectively, and so that the staff can concentrate on teaching and learning.

One of the showcase departments of the school is the English department. The English results are truly impressive: they are continually improving and their results are excellent. The teachers in this department are young and energetic, and they work hard to maintain the high levels of achievement in their subject. They divide the classes into attainment groups in each year – they select the young people very early on in their school careers, and put them into sets which focus on different materials and different ways of working to suit, they believe, the different abilities of the young people in each group.

The school leader believes passionately in mixed-ability grouping. As a younger teacher, she worked towards excellent mixed-ability group work, and was known to be successful in this. She sees good mixed-ability teaching as the outward sign of her values about equity and social justice, and she would like all the teachers in the school to share these values. However, she also believes in democratic decision-making and in encouraging her teachers to make professionally informed decisions. She works hard at professional development in the school, ensuring that as many teachers as possible access current thinking in their subject areas. She encourages the teachers to base their departmental decisions and subsequent work on such up-to-date thinking.

The school leader's dilemma with her highly successful English department, therefore, is that although they are so effective, they organise their learning and teaching in a way that she finds difficult to support. They see themselves as having the same values of high achievement for everyone, and they are convinced that the young people flourish better in groups of similar ability. The school leader thinks that teaching the young people in same-ability sets clashes with her own understandings about equality of opportunity – she is convinced that they are apt to feel labelled and to fulfil the expectations teachers have of their ability. However, the school leader has encouraged staff in the school to make autonomous but informed decisions about their departmental organisation: she has led them with equity, encouraging them to reach their own professional and informed decisions based on research and discussion. They are responding to her encouragement by introducing a way of working that clashes totally with one of her sets of values – equity – but at the same time, they are encouraged by another set of her values – those of democracy and professional development and professional autonomy.

This school leader has made the values-led decision to encourage the staff in the school to make informed decisions about their professional practice. So she is tolerating the same-ability grouped groups in English because the English department is clear that is the most successful way of teaching for them. One could ask whether she 'allows' this internal organisation because the department is so successful: would she intercede more and impose her values more if they were less successful?

It seems to me that this school leader's dilemmas include:

- Balancing her own strong sense of equity through empowerment with her English department's highly successful understandings about learning and teaching – mixed-ability teaching groups or setting according to ability?
- Whether to tell her staff how to teach, or to encourage them to research and develop their own ways of working
- Whether to define success through publicly displayed results or through harder to measure empowerment and sense of self-worth (although it should not be taken for granted that the teachers in the English department have not considered notions of empowerment and the development of self-worth)
- Whether to impose her values on the staff or to encourage them to do what they think is best for the young people.

It is necessary to examine educational settings to better appreciate emergent multiple meanings and realities related to context, time, and language. Questions to be asked are abundant. For example:

- Is it necessary for all participants involved in collaborative decision making – which often gives rise to value conflicts – to not only arrive at shared values but to begin with shared conceptualizations of the nature of values?
- How do leaders facilitate shared decision making when stakeholders subscribe to different value orientations and hold different and often subconscious interpretations of value theory?
- How can leaders facilitate the process of arriving at 'the common good'?
- What is the nature of the relationship between language and power in the role of achieving common ground?

(Leonard 1999: 252)

The following questions arise in relation to the school leader and the school described above:

1. To what extent should her beliefs about democracy override her understandings about equity and fairness?
2. To what extent should the school leader work towards resolving this conflict? Should she insist that the English department dispenses with streamed sets? Should she quietly accept their régime? Should she work towards a compromise where the younger classes are taught in mixed-ability grouping and the older ones in streamed sets? Indeed, should she even tell them that she disagrees with their chosen way of working?
3. Apart from the dilemmas posed within the school between the school leader and the English department, there is an internal conflict of values within the school leader herself. She will make her decision about imposing her beliefs or keeping quiet in order to respect a professional decision after thinking about which of her own conflicting values carries more weight: it really refines down to democracy versus equity.

It is clear that there may be a tension between the leader's values and the values of those around the leader: the values of all concerned with an institution may not be congruent, or they may hold different stakeholder interests. A basic leadership value may well influence the extent to which dissention can be accommodated. For example, one leadership value may be that everyone deserves respect, and so everybody must be heard and so the leader searches out ways to give everyone a voice. To what extent is it a leadership responsibility to bring the organisation to total agreement about values? To what extent can dissension be seen as a creative developmental force? Is it a basic leadership responsibility to ensure that different views and values are tolerated and even respected within a staff team? The tolerance of such difference models a welcoming of difference in the wider community – an important value.

One question here is whether there are universally held values which cannot tolerate dissension, or whether a universally held value is based on the tolerance of difference. Is commitment to social justice necessary and immutable in all teachers?

A principled school manager may believe that those who work in the school should have space to develop and work with their own educational values. But the same manager is committed to embedding the school's published purpose in all that happens there - how might the different sets of values be mediated? Or indeed, is there room for different sets of values in one educational organisation?

(Gold and Evans 1998: 6)

The leader should note that the bulk of collective behaviour, political or social or organizational, is devoted to and dependent upon the establishment of some sort of *modus vivendi* or working resolution of value conflict. An organization is, strictly speaking, an arrangement for conflict management through the device of super-ordinate or overriding goals.

(Hodgkinson 1991: 90)

A CAPABILITIES APPROACH

Martha Nussbaum has developed a capabilities approach to answer the question of universally held values. She addresses issues of social justice in the concrete reality of the struggles of poor women in less affluent countries. I have chosen to introduce her work because although it initially seems far removed from schools in western or affluent countries, the distance helps to strip the argument to the barest of essentials, which then clarifies the application of such issues in the west. She describes a capabilities approach.

A capabilities approach is based on:
'a bare minimum of what respect for human dignity requires ... the best approach to this idea of a basic social minimum is provided by an approach that focuses on *human capabilities*, that is, what people are actually able to do and to be – in a way informed by an intuitive idea of a life that is worthy of the dignity of the human being.'

(Nussbaum 2000: 5)

Martha Nussbaum offers a list of central human functional capabilities which she sees as providing the underpinnings of basic political principles that are embodied in constitutional guarantees. She has worked them from poor women in less affluent countries, but ensured through her argument that they are universal. I offer them here in an abbreviated form (see the box below), certain that they are globally fundamental to education and to the leadership of education. In order to do the list justice, they should be read in full.

Human capabilities

1. **Life**
Being able to live to the end of a human life of normal length

2. **Bodily health**
Being able to have good health, including reproductive health

3. **Bodily integrity**
Being able to move freely from place to place

4. **Senses, imagination and thought**
Being able to use the senses ... in a way informed and cultivated by adequate education

5. **Emotions**
Being able to have attachments to things and people outside ourselves

6. **Practical reason**
Being able to form a conception of the good and to engage in critical reflection about the planning of one's life

7. **Affiliation**
A. being able to live with and toward others ...
B. Having the social bases for self-respect and non-humiliation

8. **Other species.** Being able to live with concern for and in relation to animals, plants and the world of nature.

9. **Play**
Being able to laugh, to play, to enjoy recreational activity

10. **Control over one's environment**
A. Political. Being able to participate effectively in political choices that govern one's life ...
B. Material. Being able to hold property (both land and movable goods) not just formally but in terms of real opportunity.

(from Nussbaum 2000: 78–80)

Sources of capital funding

Although Martha Nussbaum's list of capabilities does not immediately answer the question about universal and shared values, it does offer some criteria by which to make important decisions. The measuring up of demands to criteria, and the balancing them within a hierarchy, is of course dependant on personal values, and therefore different for each of us. It may be that Martha Nussbaum is offering a bottom line below which educators should not look.

The next two chapters address questions about building and sharing values. Direct answers are not given, because no single answer would match the values and professional contexts of all school leaders. However, strategies for finding answers to these questions are given – several of them grow directly out of our research, and others are drawn from the learning conversations which take place in our courses at the Institute of Education.

6 *Strategies for building and sharing values*

This section is very practical. It lays out some suggestions for values-sharing strategies that flow from the research, reading and arguments presented earlier. It contains sets of lists that are intended as guidelines to underpin the development of those strategies. However, first I must clarify that every dimension of these strategies displays a clear example of values in practice: how firmly they are in place; who manages them; whether they are coercive or developmental; whether they demand agreement or welcome challenge – all depend on leadership values which ultimately inform school culture.

It may well be that the same leader employs different strategies, or combinations of strategies depending on how long they have been a school leader or on how the institution is organised. The strategies chosen depend on whether the leader wants to hear and be affected or changed by the professional voices around them; by how much time there is to make decisions; by how persuasive or imposed the decisions are to be; and, often, by the magnitude and the significance of the decisions to be made. Decision-making practices can be educative and developmental in themselves, they may be driven by a need for expediency or they may illustrate dysfunctional power relationships within an organisation. They should never been undertaken lightly, and a thoughtful leader ensures that the process fits the intended outcome – difficult decisions and ones which may provoke dissenting voices may be planned and handled differently from those in which less is invested in the outcome.

It is clear that the capacity for toleration of dissension is informed by values. There are leaders who welcome dissension and who see that the discussions thrown up by professional disagreements, when managed respectfully, are educative and productive. After such discussions, colleagues are more able to understand what they have decided to do, and may well have contributed to decisions about whether to do what has been requested initially, and then what to do and how to do it in a professional manner. There are also values-led leadership decisions about the extent to which all staff are involved in all decisions – there are instances when those who are leading an organisation sense that their colleagues are happy to relinquish their decision-making rights, in order to do what has been decided for them. However, it is not always easy to know which decisions colleagues wish to be deeply involved in and which they are content to leave to the leadership team. A leader needs to know staff well and to be able to read *their* political and values-led drive.

Do you know which decisions your colleagues wish to take part in, and which decisions they will happily leave to you?

In practical terms, here is a list of suggestions for some school-based activities that offer organisational opportunities for explorative and profound values discussions. To some extent, the list is informed by the research I described in the previous section. But there are also suggestions which come from my being around schools for so long:

- Effective recruitment procedures
- Staff induction
- Well-managed staff meetings
- Agreed and active in-house communication systems (printed and online)
- Productive continuing professional development – 'Learning Conversations'
- Developing the relationship of the Leadership Team to the rest of the school.

> Can you add to this list? It is certainly not an exhaustive list, and creative school leaders have many other ways of encouraging educative discussions.

EFFECTIVE RECRUITMENT PROCEDURES

Several of the school leaders to whom we spoke told us about developing their own staff team and about choosing staff who shared their values. In 'Articulating leadership values in action' we spoke to Mr A., who told us:

> *'I've been lucky now, I've selected about 80 per cent of the staff. At selection, I make it clear what is the vision and the ethos. They must want to work at [this school].'*

So, staff recruitment is central to team building and to developing a shared set of values in a school. But in parts of the UK, and in other education systems, there is little freedom about the way staff are recruited. Procedures are laid down by local authorities or, in centralised education systems, they are managed by the Ministry or Directorate of Education. It may be that there are many applicants for each post advertised, or that there is a severe shortage of suitable applicants. It may be that teachers are drafted into posts by central offices, or that some posts bring higher salaries with them or are in more favourable surroundings than others – recruitment to different schools has entered the market place in many countries and may be affected by market principles.

However, in many organisations, there is more freedom in recruiting new members of staff than appears at first glance. In the first place, the recruitment procedure should be underpinned by such principles as those summarised in the Nolan Report (see p. 9). This would mean that the decisions taken

- **are in the public interest** (not for financial or material benefit),
- are made with **integrity** (not influenced by obligations to outside individuals or organisations),
- are made with **objectivity** (on clear merit),
- show clear **accountability** (are able to undergo appropriate answerability),
- are **open to scrutiny** (can be explained, and reasons can be given for the decisions made)
- are made **honestly** (with appropriate declaration of private or conflicting interests)
- show clear **leadership** (even if they are difficult, they stand up to scrutiny and are exemplars of ethical public life).

Sometimes, these principles can be compromised by a different, but overriding, set of principles: if there is a shortage of applicants for a post it may be that the school leaders will either invite people to apply, or ask others to invite specific people to apply for a post. In this case, the principle of ensuring that good learning and teaching takes place in a school may override the principles laid out by the Nolan Committee. But whatever recruitment procedure is chosen, it must be chosen after clearly weighing up different ethical dimensions.

Even if a post is centrally controlled, a school leader can influence the description of the post to be filled, so that the new recruit fits or changes the space in the organisation. For example, in the Inner London Education Authority in the 1980s, there were attempts to develop recruitment procedures that were built upon understandings of equal opportunities. Since then, organisations have adopted and adapted various forms and understandings of equity into their recruitment procedures. An ethical recruitment procedure is based on clear values which usually ensure that the most appropriate person is appointed, through inclusive procedures which take account of issues of equity. The Nolan principles are alive in the following recruitment procedure, which is still effective when adapted to appropriate frameworks.

1. A panel is drawn up partly from the team to be rebuilt, and partly from people outside the immediate team but connected to it – governors or colleagues from another part of or a similar organisation. The panel will include a representative cross section of people – in terms of gender, ethnicity and so on. They will be working together throughout the procedure (drawing up the job description, the person specification, the long list, the short list, the interview questions, and then contributing to the interview itself).

2. The process will be chaired by someone whose responsibility it is to make sure that everyone on the panel has a voice and that the process is fair.

3. An exit interview at this stage will provide an opportunity for the previous incumbent to offer advice about improving the job in the future.

4. The job description, drawn up by the panel, is focused on the job to be done: it entails a clear assessment of changes in the work, and takes account of the work rather than the desired person – this ensures that there is not a simple duplication of the previous job description or person specification. It is carefully described in the language and values of the organisation – it fits the culture.

5. The chair, especially, ensures that the language of the job description, of the advertisement, and the person specification matches the work to be done, and that the job is advertised in an appropriate place. Some job descriptions use such powerfully focused language – that of sport or of driven success – that some significant applicants may not find the job description attractive.

6. The long- and short-listing criteria are drawn up from the job description and person specification. These processes usually take place when the panel sits together in the same room, a set time before the interview date. It is easier to focus on the criteria if a grid is drawn up and duplicated, and used by each member of the panel.

7. Usually, all candidates who are invited to interview have shown through their application that they reach the published criteria for the job – if they do not reach the criteria, they should not be interviewed, thus making sure that the process does not raise false hopes.

8. Before the interview begins, questions based on the job description and person specification sent previously to each interviewee are developed within the panel. The questions are shared out among the interview panel so that everyone speaks – no one remains silent – and the chair makes sure that the process runs smoothly.

9. The chair makes it clear that the interview is a two-way process, and that the interviewee is making choices too. This means that interviewees are put at their ease so that they will interview as well as possible; they are offered the opportunity to ask questions as well as answer them; and so the most appropriate person will be offered the post.

10. The panel members, having used a common grid on which to mark 'met', 'partially met' and 'not met' about answers to questions, will make their decisions as soon as possible after all the interviews are completed.

11. After the chosen interviewee has accepted the post, the unsuccessful applicants are told as soon as possible, and are offered feedback on the interview if they so wish.

This procedure is an example of a values-led recruitment procedure. It may be changed or added to, but basically it pays attention to the power relations involved in a typical recruitment process, and it is a suggested way of ensuring that those power relations do not stop the appointment of the most appropriate applicant. Successful interviewing procedures are the key to building and maintaining a team which develops and delivers principled school leadership.

> Can you remember your own interview for the post you hold at the moment? Did you feel free to speak and to ask questions? Were you able to think clearly and to show yourself to be someone you wanted to be? Did the procedure seem fair to you?

STAFF INDUCTION

The introduction of new members of staff is a key way for leaders to develop their own values-led culture – the latter are able to form their own team, rather than working with the team left by the previous school leader. But staff selection alone is not enough: it is important to design staff induction procedures to be as supportive and enabling as possible. They are set up to make sure that new members of staff and staff new to their roles can contribute to the life of the school as usefully as possible, and as early as possible.

If new team members or team leaders come into the organisation from outside, they have to juggle being new and learning the official and unofficial structures of the organisation with the need to be effective and productive as soon as possible, while at the same time being judged by all about them. If the new team member is promoted from within the organisation, the period of adjustment is still complicated, but this time they may need guidance to peel away from previous alliances and friendships without arousing conflict or sabotage, and they usually need support to operate differently, often to take on another perspective which is broader than before.

Most writing about team dynamics, especially the life cycle of teams (Gold 1998: 23) shows how carefully the entry of new team members is to be managed, if they are to contribute to the principled operation of a school. The normal life cycle of a team – forming, storming, norming, performing, adjourning and mourning (see Gold 1998: 23–4) – can be interrupted by the entry of even one new team member. If an established team is not well led, new team members may be blamed for upsetting the *status quo* rather than receiving welcome for the different ways of operating they might bring with them. Apart from informing new team members about the ways of the organisation, introducing them to the rest of the school, helping them to develop a management and leadership which suits both them and the organisation and apart from helping them to frame their leadership goals, the appropriate team needs to adapt to them. The existing team needs to be ready to operate differently in order to make the best use of the talents, skills, experience and attributes the new team member brings with them.

So, induction has to be planned on many levels; leading staff induction is a delicate activity, but one which is key to creative schools. How might it be done better? What curriculum should it include? The decisions about what and whom to include in the induction process, and indeed, how to do it, are informed by values.

Some points to think about when planning an induction programme for new members of staff:

- The induction programme is a clear and immediate indicator to new staff about whose opinions are valued in the school, and about who is invited to influence decisions. How significant is the first induction meeting and the induction programme? Who is invited to talk to new members of staff?
- Are the new colleagues are as well informed as possible? What information is key? For example, how accurate are the handbooks and flowcharts which introduce the school to new staff? Do they describe the formal or the informal decision-making channels? And, indeed, how important is it that new staff know about the informal decision-making channels? And if they know about them, should they be encouraged to use them? And if they begin to use them, how then how does everybody access the formal decision-making routes and thus have a voice in organisational decisions?
- How much time is given over to the induction period? How long are new members of staff allowed to feel that they are new and excused for not knowing how the school operates? How long can they expect extra support for their newness?
- Are new staff set up with mentors at the beginning of their induction period?
- Are they given the opportunity to ask questions and to make sense of the whole organisation? Do established staff listen to questions from new staff – questions which are often important ones about the way the school runs and which can cut through the unofficial and archival ways the school has been running.

The tone and attitude with which new members of staff are welcomed and encouraged to speak is part of the culture of the school, and may be set by the leadership team. The way newness is handled gives a powerful message to new staff about their place in the organisation, and the extent to which their opinions are valued, or whether they are to fit in without questioning the usual operation of the organisation.

Ms E., in our paper 'Articulating leadership values in action', was quite clear about the importance of the induction period in which to transmit her values about leadership:

I have always taken the appointment of staff very seriously. I have always talked to those I am appointing and some people don't like what I stand for, because I am not interested in authoritarianism. I am interested in real empowerment and that is very frightening for some people. I have had some teachers who have come here, as with two deputy heads of maths [scale] B they talked, turned round and ran.

(Campbell *et al.* 2003: 211)

WELL-MANAGED STAFF MEETINGS Staff meetings are the spaces in schools which offer a clear public display of leadership values. When doing the research for our case studies (Gold *et al.* 2003), the whole research team agreed to attend as many staff meetings as we could, in order to see examples of leadership in action. We wrote:

Frequently we were told about the importance of meetings as decision-making spaces and about the amount of information made available to staff. It seems to us that meetings are the visible manifestation of a school leader's values system: clear ideals about respecting, transforming, developing and including staff can be evidenced by the importance given to meetings in a school and by the way meetings are run.

School leaders and other staff in our case studies gave us many examples of how meetings and information were seen as important: in one special school, we heard how teamwork was fostered and facilitated through meetings of the whole staff, team meetings and a programme of individual discussions between the school leader and all members of staff. The free flow of information within the school was referred to by many members of staff and was seen as contributing to the spirit of togetherness and the inhibition of any feeling of 'them and us'. In this school, good communication was not left to chance – there were systems in place such as the staff-room notice board, the circulation of minutes of meetings and the weekly staff briefings in order to ensure that information and ideas were freely shared.

In a large secondary school, we observed a woman school leader showing her respect for her colleagues through the way she ran meetings: she constantly invited them to contribute their views, building consensus round the discussion and generally building agreement through the discussion.

(Gold *et al.* 2003: 130–1)

It is not always necessary for a school leader to chair staff meetings, but it is clear that serious preparation should take place for such meetings in order to ensure maximum usefulness. And of course, not all meetings are set up for the whole staff. Most staff attend several different types of meetings each week, and they can feel welcomed, active, passive or marginalised in different ones, sometimes run by the same leader. However, staff are very clear about whether the meetings they have attended are worthwhile, and whether they wish to attend and contribute to such meetings in future.

Managing meetings   It may be helpful use the following questions as a checklist about every meeting that school and other staff are called to, as all meetings pass many unspoken messages on to those who take part in them:

- What is the purpose of this meeting: exchange of information, decision-making, professional development, planning, consultation, team building? It may be any or a combination of any of these purposes, but the meeting will be organised differently depending on the planned outcome.
- Is the purpose of the meeting clear to those who are to take part in it? And are all those who are invited to take part the appropriate people to contribute to the proposed outcome?
- How is the room set up?
- Which underpinning values does the leader intend to transmit at the meeting? If it is about swift and decisive leadership, what information is necessary beforehand? Are the team members informed enough to offer fast responses? If it is for an educative and profound discussion about issues that might change the way the school operates, is this clear? How has information been disseminated? How is it to be organised so that the 'right' people can speak and be heard? Is the meeting run in such a way as to encourage everyone present to speak? Are all shown respect and allowed, or even encouraged to speak, and do they think that they have been listened to?
- Are there clear signs of a well-chaired and respectful meeting? Does it begin and end on time? Are decisions and outcomes reached, and clear to all who are there? Does everyone have a voice? Is discussion shared in a rational debate? Has the chair paid attention to the process, or had they already decided to drive through the outcome they desired before the beginning of the meeting? Does summing-up occur when required, and does the meeting draw to a suitable close?
- The level of democratic decision-making or swift and decisive decision-making can be gauged from: the management of the agenda (who has access to it and who can add to it); how the minutes of previous meetings including action-points are handled (how accurate they are and who wrote them). How long before and after meetings is relevant

paperwork accessible to those involved? Is the paperwork useful and does it contribute to the information flow? And, is the paperwork accessible to all whether they attend the meeting or not – can everyone in the organisation find out about decisions which affect their work, even if they were not part of the initial decision-making process?

It is worthwhile thinking about the questions listed above when running meetings – they are key spaces for school staff, and staff welcome or dislike meetings depending on how useful people find them.

As our research shows, meetings are a very public place in which to display leadership values. Such values as clear leadership (by displaying how decisions are made), who has a voice in the decision-making, who is respected, the direction and importance of information flow, and whether the school is educative for staff as well as young people, can be 'read' in a staff meeting.

AGREED AND ACTIVE IN-HOUSE COMMUNICATION SYSTEMS (PRINTED AND ONLINE)

In-school communications systems were formerly focused mainly on print – on staff bulletins and on school newsletters – or on staff meetings. But at present, it seems that the technological dimension of leadership is a fast developing one, and one which the British government wishes to support. We were fascinated to record how one school leader in one of our research schools used his in-house communication systems. Those members of his staff to whom we spoke were delighted by the way he set up laptop computers for each of them with school information systems. These included planning sheets, school end-of-year reports and annual reviews (the school catered for young people with special needs). The same school leader read widely professionally, and downloaded and disseminated articles or resumés of articles in order to keep his staff up to date and informed. He was excited about learning and about continuing to learn, and he transmitted this excitement to his staff by technological means – both online and by print. His staff was pleased by this.

There are some key questions to be answered when encouraging the wider spread of information management systems and the general development of technology in the management of schools. Although technology is exciting and often opens doors that have previously seemed locked, and although it often means that some tasks can be carried out faster or with a more professional flourish, concerns to do with the work–life balance of teachers in connection with the wider use of technology are slowly emerging. Answers to these questions can be found in fundamental understandings about how much time a senior professional might be expected to spend in work, where that work is done, and how important it is to be *seen* to be in regular connection with school. So this sub-section comes with a health warning which acknowledges the excitement and enabling aspect of the use of technology in management systems, but which points out the dangers of blurring the boundaries between work and home, and the added professional expectations about access to information that such technology brings with it.

This argument is taken further by two research findings we took from our project for the National College for School Leadership, published in 2002. When we were asked by the NCSL to look into the 'current state of school leadership in England', we were collecting 'baseline' data about school leadership for the DfES and the NCSL. Our research design made use of a mixture of different data-collecting techniques, including case studies, interviews, telephone discussions, face-to-face focus groups, questionnaires, and on-line focus groups. Our research questions included:

> *how different leaders understand their leadership roles and the value they place on them; the general attractiveness of particular school leadership positions; the quality of people's preparedness for leadership positions; the degree to which principals or headteachers regard themselves as belonging to an evidence-based profession; the*

sources of ideas and inspiration that school leaders turn to in the course of undertaking their work; the degree to which ICT and the world wide web is used to both access and contribute to best practice evidence; and, the level of school leaders' awareness of the remit and role of the NCSL, and their perceptions of how they might become involved in its work.

(Earley *et al.* 2002: 128)

We were struck both by the times at which participants chose to respond to online discussions and by their comments about what they saw as the bureaucracy of school leadership.

The times at which the online discussions took place

We were a little uncomfortable about who responded to the online discussion and when they did so. It was clear that this happened after all other school work was done, either at weekends or late in the evening. Of course, this was in response to a research project, rather than an integral part of the task of leading a school. However, it did show us that there is a temptation to see online tasks as added on to other, face-to-face, leadership tasks. And we wondered whether such tasks were completed in leisure or private time, thus disturbing the work–life balance that many school leaders struggle to work towards.

School leaders who embrace technology as a means of easing pressure on the paperwork of leadership are to be warned about the response times expected, and encouraged to see technology as a useful tool rather than a demand that requires an immediate response.

Bureaucracy

We asked middle leaders whether they were considering senior leadership roles, and if they were not, why not. We were struck most forcefully by the number of middle leaders who were keen to avoid what they saw as the overpowering bureaucracy which came with senior leadership. Those who were disinclined to apply for senior leadership gave their expectation of bureaucratic overload as one of their main reasons. They were afraid of being weighed down by paperwork, which they saw as a problem for senior leaders. We suspected that some senior leaders passed down the bureaucracy to middle leaders, but it was outside the remit of this research project to verify our suspicions.

So, given these two provisos – timing and overload – it is clear that technological information flows are seen as valuable. But there are other ways of informing colleagues about the working of the organisation. The chosen information conduit should be accessible and easy to use, and should ensure that its use makes life easier, rather than adding to an already over-burdened workload.

In-house communication

There is also a question about 'in-house communication' – who is 'in-house'? Some school leaders see governors as part of the school, and others see parents as close members of the school community. This discussion widens the scope of in-house communication systems, but it is one which will change and expand as technology extends to make communication easier.

PRODUCTIVE CONTINUING PROFESSIONAL DEVELOPMENT – 'LEARNING CONVERSATIONS'

This is not the place for a treatise on continuing professional development. Rather, I offer an opportunity to link a commitment to continuing professional development with some specific school-based opportunities in which to build and share values. Often, professional development is seen as a formal activity which demands time, money and careful planning. A senior member of staff holds the responsibility for professional development within the school, and there is a specific fund attached to it (and much more if senior leaders manage to make successful bids for linked development funding). It is true that a formal, well planned whole-staff professional development session offers an excellent opportunity for many people to work creatively towards negotiating and developing further a shared professional culture. Well delivered whole-school and departmental professional development sessions work well, and are vital to the life of a school. But *continuing* professional development works best in an on-going learning culture in which different forms of professional development take place – it is the culture which informs a professional development strategy for a school. It is the framework within which many different types of professional development are set up: some of them long-term, some of them short-term, some involving everyone, others more specifically targeted, but all based on values around developing and supporting professional attitudes and activities.

It is not always necessary to spend a great deal of money and time to encourage continuous professional development. An educative school which pays attention to learning and teaching for everyone within the school community buzzes with discussions and thought-provoking arguments, as well as planned formal learning opportunities. Such discussions take a little time, but are inexpensive. They only need planning in that people who work in the school are encouraged to take part in them and have thought about them. It becomes part of the school community to have productive discussions in which people listen carefully to each other.

The most educative activity that those who manage the learning of young people can take part in is ensuring that everyone takes part in constructive discussions – described by Brookfield as Learning Conversations. The most productive times that beginning teachers or those who are working with challenging young people, or those who wish to change the way learning and teaching is happening in their classrooms can find to develop further is usually through careful conversations with colleagues, mentors or tutors. It is in these conversations that basic values and understandings about power relations and about learning and teaching can be explored.

---

1. Good conversations are reciprocal and involving:
in a good conversation, the participants are continually involved in the process; they are either talking or listening. Developing critical thinking is a process in which listening and contributing are of equal importance.

2. The course of good conversations cannot be anticipated:
when we begin to ask people to identify assumptions underlying their habitual ways of thinking and learning, we do not know exactly how they are going to respond.

3. Good conversations entail diversity and agreement:
a measure of diversity, disagreement, and challenge is central to helping people to think critically. Unless we accept that people have views very different from ours, and that a multiplicity of interpretations of practically every idea or action is possible, we will be unable to contemplate alternatives in our own thoughts and actions.

(Brookfield 1987: 38–241)

Take, for an example, a teacher who has just finished teaching a difficult class, and who is sitting in the staff room distressed and depressed. In many staff rooms, this teacher would be offered a cup of coffee and soothing words about how awful the class is normally. The discussion would be repetitive and the teacher may be encouraged to forget the incident. A learning conversation, on the other hand would, of course, begin with commiserations and comfort, but would perhaps take place in a more private place where participants could focus on the discussion. It would include some challenge, from both participants:

'What happened then, exactly?'

'Why do you think that happened?'

'What happened next?'

'Why are you asking these questions?'

'Because I really want to know and to try to work out what was really happening....

What do you think would happen if....? Have you thought about beginning the class this way? How can I help you in future?'

This is really an explorative conversation, where neither person knows the answers, and both are listening and talking in turn, and both are moving forward towards suggestions which fit the person learning to manage the class differently. But it moves forward – it is important to make sure that the conversation does not become stuck or repetitive, and that it focuses on the development of new teaching strategies.

Learning conversations challenge the usual power relations within a hierarchy of a school, because they are based on the premise that there is no single answer, that no one is right, and that challenge is welcome. The key responsibility within such a conversation is the need to ensure that it moves forward, and that respectful learning takes place as a result of it.

DEVELOPING THE RELATIONSHIP OF THE LEADERSHIP TEAM TO THE REST OF THE SCHOOL

In the schools in our research, it was clear that most of the school leaders paid attention to the relationship between the leadership team and the other members of the school community. Members of the senior leadership teams themselves and other members of staff commented to us about this special relationship and they did so in more than one school. Such careful attention paid to this key relationship shows a profound understanding of power relationships and of their affects on other people.

Leading the senior leadership team so that it is creative, productive and leaderly, and at the same time ensuring that the rest of the staff respects the team, demands a very fine and sensitive understanding of interpersonal relations. It is not always easy to know when colleagues will expect to be included in profound discussions about the learning and teaching activities in which they are involved, and when they will look to the leadership team to make decisions for them. And it could be that different colleagues expect different levels of consultation at different times.

We were intrigued by the sensitivity with which school leaders were able to encourage the leadership team to be decisive and yet were able to hear voices from the staff. It was clearly a leadership skill which allowed the leaders to gauge the right balance. And this skill is informed by an understanding of group dynamics, a belief that most staff are professionally committed, and a faith that what other colleagues have to say is worth hearing. So, a school leader must not only develop that faith in the professionalism of colleagues within the leadership team, but has to lead that team to be worthy of the respect of the rest of the staff.

It was possible to see different sets of leadership values displayed by the different approaches the school leaders in our research took towards the relationship between the senior leadership team and the rest of the school. Mainly, we were struck by the way these leaders, who had all been seen by Ofsted inspectors to be particularly successful, seemed to merge at times into their leadership teams. They took responsibility for the actions of the team while sometimes finding it difficult to trace the evolution and development of ideas within the team.

In this section I have described some practical ways in which values may be developed, displayed or shared. The strategies laid out here became apparent in our research, but there are many more such strategies. School leaders display their values throughout their working days, from their entry to the school premises in the morning (what vehicle, where they park, what time the day begins, what they wear, how colleagues are greeted, how young people are greeted). Sometimes they are conscious of this display of values, but sometimes, when stressed, they find it more difficult to be the leader they would like to be.

Which of your professional actions displayed your educational values today? Are you satisfied with this?

Leaders finding space to articulate

their own values

I have referred throughout the book to reading and research about school leadership and values, and I have offered practical suggestions for working with the values in schools. This section is written to provide support for the school leaders with whom responsibility for articulating organisational values ultimately rests.

Most school leaders who wish to be led by their values are hard-pressed to ensure that they have sufficient opportunity to take time for reflection about their own practice. That time would allow them to make sense of current challenges, and to decide on a course of action which is in accord with their underpinning principles of leadership in education. Such reflection time is necessary for all members of staff, and the previous section recounts some strategies for the whole school. But it is often difficult for school leaders to make time for their own reflection in the busy life of a school: in greedy or busy organisations, it is difficult to prioritise thinking time and to give permission not to be continually outwardly and obviously active or productive. Even if the culture of the school offers such time to the rest of the staff, some school leaders cannot easily allow themselves such time.

Here are a few suggestions for ways in which a school leader might safeguard their own time for reflection:

- Being mentored
- Mentoring others
- Not responding immediately
- Reflective writing
- The 'five whys'.

Can you add to this list?

BEING MENTORED

David Clutterbuck writes that mentoring schemes in different parts of the world are based on fundamentally different assumptions about the role and nature of mentoring. He quotes the definition given by his colleague, Jenny Sweeney:

Mentoring is a partnership between two people built upon trust. It is a process in which the mentor offers ongoing support and development opportunities to the mentee. Addressing issues and blockages identified by the mentee, the mentor offers guidance, counselling and support in the form of pragmatic and objective assistance. Both share a common purpose of developing a strong two-way relationship.

(Clutterbuck 2001: 5–6)

Good mentoring is not about giving recipes for educational success. Good mentoring for school leaders is not set up to give school leadership advice. Mentoring arrangements, when they work successfully, offer the opportunity to reflect with rigour on such issues as those raised in this publication. The mentoring process is premised on the same guidelines as Brookfield's Learning Conversations – the mentoring conversation works towards the person mentored reaching a conclusion about leadership activities that best fits the organisation, the values, the context and the issue.

It is often easier to set up mentoring systems for other staff within an educational organisation than it is to arrange suitable mentoring for the head of the organisation. This is perhaps because it is easier to spend time on such arrangements for other people than for oneself. It is clear that school leaders must give themselves permission to seek out suitable arrangements for their own mentoring, so that they create the opportunity for a constructive thinking space and so that they model such an arrangement for those they lead.

In the UK, some local authorities make plans for, or fund the setting up of, mentoring arrangements for new school leaders. These activities could mean that a school leader has regular contact with a neighbouring school leader who has been in post longer and who is therefore likely to understand better the task of school leadership within that authority. It could also be that a school leader uses professional development funding to pay for a set of mentors appropriate to different aspects of the leadership task: a leadership mentor and a business mentor and so on. In this case, the challenge is that the school leader would have to compartmentalise the discussions so that relevant discussions are taken to the appropriate mentor who may well not be in education, and the overall coherence is left to the school leader. But in return for overseeing the coherence, the different mentors would offer high quality mentoring in different fields of expertise.

There is an added dimension when the school leader comes from an under-represented social group. Their understanding and experience of power mean that they do not have the same approach to leadership as the dominant UK discourse of leadership and power, and it may be difficult to match them with an appropriate mentor within the education service. For example, Marianne Coleman's current research for the National College of School Leaders shows that in the north of England there is an under-representation of women leaders of secondary schools. I have heard such women talk about their loneliness and lack of role model in their region when trying to lead the school in a way that they feel most comfortable with. Such women may find helpful and supportive mentoring from similarly senior women, but there are not enough women in senior positions in education in their region. It may be advisable therefore to look for women mentors who are in similar positions in other public services – for example in the social services, local government, the police or higher education. These women may well share some of the same leadership problems and possibilities, and so will understand the explorative conversations that need to take place.

However leadership mentoring is set up, it can offer an excellent opportunity to refer back to values and to make sure that, wherever possible, leadership actions are informed by such values. A school leader can probably only have such conversations in a calm and thoughtful environment, and with a mentor who is committed to confidentiality and to focusing on exploration and learning.

MENTORING OTHERS

In an effective mentoring relationship the mentor will learn as much from the explorative conversations as the person they are mentoring.

There are already some opportunities embedded in the education system for explorative and well led conversations which are akin to mentorship to take place in school. For example, within present arrangements for performance management in English schools, school leaders tend to have individual interviews with their senior staff in order to set and review professional targets. These interviews, although led by more senior people (or line managers), have an aspect of mentoring about them: the subject of the interview is encouraged to set their own targets, with some support, and to make sure that they fit their own developmental needs and the needs of the organisation. However, such discussions may eventually be linked to salary increments. So, although they focus carefully on one person and their professional activities, as mentoring does, they are not entirely as free of judgement as a true mentoring relationship should be.

School leaders may set up opportunities within school to mentor members of staff, or they may offer their services to colleagues outside the school, as in the previous section. Mentoring offers a great opportunity for reflection for both mentor and person mentored. The school leader who acts as mentor to others will find ample opportunity to reflect on their own practice within the mentoring relationship. While working with others to match their actions to values and to articulate their educative values, the mentor will automatically find themselves searching back to their own motivations and driving forces. Although there is little opportunity to display these basic understandings within the mentoring relationship, the discussions allow space for self-examination in order to make professional and practical linkages for other people.

NOT RESPONDING IMMEDIATELY

Being a little hotheaded myself, I am always impressed by those who take time to make up their mind about professional decisions. I know that ultimately their well judged actions will be more principled than mine because they have taken the opportunity to reflect on their values and to link their subsequent actions to those values.

When I first became a pastoral leader in an inner-London comprehensive school, I strode down corridors almost manically, sorting out problems and responding immediately to demands and to colleagues' requests for support. I prided myself on the speed of my responses and on my empathy, and I told myself that I was being firmer and more decisive than was my normal inclination, but this was how I saw good leadership then: I was doing what I thought people expected of me.

However, I soon realised that my speedy responses sometimes resulted in inappropriate outcomes. When I thought back over the chains of action, I was often puzzled by my part in them. I was making real mistakes in the way I was responding to people. I was much more punitive than my normal inclination, and I become conscious that my judgement was unclear, clouded by emotions that I could not recognise. So I slowed down a little, and took time to think about my own values and understandings about leadership in education. In slowing down, I realised that I was beginning to listen to my colleagues more carefully, and that I was then taking time to think about they were really saying to me and about my subsequent actions. As part of that slowing down, I found myself thinking about the strong emotions that colleagues displayed when, for example, they talked about challenging circumstances in their classrooms. Because I had been acting so quickly, I was reacting to those strong emotions, rather than my own, and I was making inappropriate decisions which were not linked with my own values. It was as though I was acting out of *their* anger and distress, as a consequence of *their* judgement rather than my own.

Subsequently, I learned to listen carefully to my colleagues, then to try to untangle my own emotional and professional responses from their responses. After doing so, I would speak to them to agree a negotiated plan of action linked with my values and a shared learning conversation. I found that my colleagues did not necessarily want me to react to them immediately. Rather, they often seemed to want to use my listening ear as a repository for their difficult and challenging responses to difficult and challenging circumstances. Often, it was enough for me to hear what they had to say. I listened, then asked questions, then we learnt together what action was appropriate, as we worked it out in conjunction with our values about education.

I realised that I needed to acknowledge that challenging behaviour often left teachers with uncomfortable feelings. It was important, after acknowledging those feelings, to work out a calm and agreed plan of action. My colleagues did not need immediate responses as long as they knew that I was listening and working out a response. Since my time as a pastoral leader, the task of school leadership seems to have become more pressured, with many more external and internal demands on school leaders. But it is still important to take time to react – to be sure not to respond immediately.

It is clear that school leaders need to take time to think, and to allow strong feelings to subside. When the feelings are apportioned where they belong, and when the feelings become less powerful, it is easier to make rational plans. The leadership skill here is to listen and to be seen to be listening, but take some time to think about subsequent actions – not to respond immediately.

The comments above relate most clearly to challenges from inside a school, but the same principle applies to external pressures. Our research showed that those school leaders who allowed themselves time to think about constantly shifting external demands were more likely to make them fit into their organisation's strategic plans.

REFLECTIVE WRITING

There are different ways of making sure of that reflective space. In the episode I describe above, I used learning conversations and discussions with my colleagues to reflect on the link between our values and our actions. In the national and international leadership courses and programmes on which I work, we introduce the idea of a reflective journal. Ideally, I give participants an attractive notebook which is small enough to fit into a pocket or handbag, and large enough to write in comfortably. We encourage people to write in the notebook (which is private – never shared) at different times during the workshop. I often stop at the end of a section of the workshop or class, and suggest that participants take two minutes to note anything they do not want to forget about the session we have just finished.

We hope the habit of writing in the notebooks will grow, so that people are writing in between sessions, making connections between the workshops and their professional experience. Our intention is to help people to begin to write reflectively in order to use their notebooks to make sense of their experiences, and to link their learning to their professional lives, and their values.

Many participants begin to write in the journals, and to use such writing as a reflective tool, although they doubt whether they will sustain such activity when they are back in school. We are aware that there are many different ways of carving out and embedding the reflective space in daily life. We offer reflective writing as one useful tool, in the hope that it will become a habit.

THE 'FIVE WHYS'

I often ask people who are doing leadership courses with me to see whether they can articulate the leadership principles underpinning their chosen actions. Although principles are not necessarily values, they are linked, and this activity is a difficult but profoundly moving one.

I worked with Peter Karstanje, a colleague from the Netherlands, who taught me that one way of getting to basic principles is to ask the five whys. This means that each time we develop a statement to explain a leadership action, we ask 'Why?' and then 'Why?' again, as if moving down to a more profound layer of understanding. I was taught to ask 'why?' five times, until we got to a final layer to which there was no longer an answer to 'why?' Then we had reached the underpinning principle.

I have found Peter Karstanje's five whys to be a creative and useful way of articulating my values, while trying to link them to my values.

In this concluding section, I have offered a small selection of activities, which offer a school leader the opportunity to reach through layers of action and response to get to underpinning values. I have tried to suggest ways of articulating values which fit with life in school, both in timing and in the attention needed. Basically, however, school leaders must give themselves and those around them time and permission to work out why they are doing what they are doing, and then to communicate the values they articulate to each other.

References

Begley, P. (2003) 'In pursuit of authentic school leadership practices'. In P. Pegley and O. Johansson (eds) *The Ethical Dimensions of School Leadership*. Dordrecht/London: Kluwer.

Braithwaite, E.R. (1959) *To Sir With Love*. London: Coronet Books (1993).

Bottery, M. (1992) *The Ethics of Educational Values*. London: Cassell.

Brookfield, S.A. (1987) *Developing Critical Thinkers*. Milton Keynes: Open University Press.

Campbell, C., Gold, A. and Lunt, I. (2003) 'Articulating leadership values in action: conversations with school leaders'. *International Journal Leadership in Education* 6, 3, July–September.

Clutterbuck, D. (2001) *Everyone Needs a Mentor: Fostering talent at work* (3rd edition). London: Chartered Institute of Personnel and Development.

Earley, P., Evans, J., Gold, A., Collarbone, P. and Halpin, D. (2002) *Establishing the Current State of School Leadership*. London: DfES.

Gold, A. (1998) *Head of Department*. London: Cassell.

Gold, A. and Evans, J. (1998) *Reflecting on School Management*. London: Falmer.

Gold, A., Evans, J., Earley, P., Halpin, D. and Collarbone, P. (2003) 'Principled principals? Values-driven leadership: evidence from ten case studies of "outstanding" school leaders'. *Educational Management and Administration* 31, 2.

Gunter, H. (2001) *Leaders and Leadership in Education*. London: Paul Chapman.

Hodgkinson, C. (1991) *Educational Leadership: The moral art*. Albany: State University of New York Press.

Hofstede, G. (1994) *Cultures and Organizations*. London: HarperCollins Business.

Leonard, P. (1999) 'Future directions'. In P. Begley and Leonard (eds) *The Values of Educational Administration* London: Falmer Press.

National College for School Leadership (NCSL) (2002) Professional Qualification for Headship, development materials pack. *Development Stage Unit 1.1: Developing a strategic educational vision*. Nottingham: NCSL.

Nolan Committee (1995) *First Report of the Committee on Standards in Public Life*. London: The Stationery Office.

Nolan Report (Summary) Online. Available HTTP: http://www.archive.official-documents.co.uk/document/parlment/nolan/nolan.htm (accessed 30 July 2004).

Nussbaum, M.C. (2000) *Women and Human Development*. Cambridge: Cambridge University Press.

Ofsted (2003) *Inspecting Schools: Framework for inspecting school*. London: Ofsted. Online. Available HTTP://www.ofsted.gov.uk/publications/docs/3266.pdf (accessed 17 September 2004).

Oldroyd, D., Elsner, D. and Poster, C. (1996) *Educational Management Today: A concise dictionary and guide.*. London: Paul Chapman Publishing

Rousseau, J.-J. (1762) *Émile*, ed. Peter Jimack. London: Phoenix (1993).

Shute, N. (1957) *On the Beach*. London: House of Stratus (2000).

Steedman, C. (1985) 'Prisonhouses'. *Feminist Review* 20, Summer.

Wright, N. (2001) 'Leadership, "bastard leadership" and managerialism: confronting twin paradoxes in the Blair education project'. *Educational Management and Administration* 29, 3.

—— (2003) 'Principled "Bastard" Leadership?' *Educational Management and Administration* 31, 2.